JAMES SYCAMORE

Recruit yourself into your dream job

Hints, tips and advice to help you be more attractive to employers, and secure your dream job.

This book was professionally typeset on Reedsy.
Find out more at reedsy.com

Contents

1

INTRODUCTION

Hi there, firstly I want to say a BIG thank you for buying the book. This is the first step in your journey to securing your dream job!

It's SO exciting for me to share my experience, hints, tips and advice to assist you in putting your best foot forward and help you along your journey to securing your dream position. It's what I do day in, day out, and I love it!

A bit about me...I grew up just outside Twickenham in a town called Whitton, South West London, and moved to Melbourne 12 years ago where I met my amazing partner, and we started growing our family of 3 wonderful kids and a dog. I'd like to say I'm a people person, but deep down I'm somewhat of an introvert, and I love to play lots of different sports from golf and basketball through to rock climbing and gymnastics, a strange mix I know.

Work wise, I've been an agency recruiter for 15+ years in London and here in Melbourne, and have helped 1000's of people secure their dream jobs, and I aim to be able to do the same for you!

I will add that, but I'm sure it's not what you're expecting, I have had many experiences over the years where people assume that it's my job, and ours as agency recruiters, to do all the heavy lifting without the person having to do anything. Sadly, this isn't the case.

I won't claim to have a golden ticket to secure your dream job, however, having been a recruitment agency specialist for many many years and assisting so many people into their dream jobs, you're in good hands. And following these steps will improve your chances by a HUGE amount.

I will also add that this may slightly vary from country to country, and company to company, and people of course, due to differences in approach and/or preferences, so please adapt the following advice to suit the process/preference and differences accordingly.

2

BEFORE YOU START LOOKING FOR A NEW JOB

THE WHY?

Are you really wanting a new job? Are you ready for a new job? Or did you just have a bad day/week? Or is there something with your team/manager?

Lists, who doesn't like a good list. List the reasons you are thinking of a new job, here are a few examples:

- You're not happy and hate getting up for work in the morning
- No career advancement opportunities
- Toxic culture, team or manager/s
- You're finding the job/tasks easy and you're not feeling challenged
- $'s - You're underpaid for what you do/against the market
- You've thought and imagined quitting, on multiple occasions
- Unethical ways of working
- Underappreciated
- You can't be yourself at work

<u>PRO's & CON's</u>

Make a list of all the Pro's and Con's of a new job within a new company, or even if it's within the same company but with a new team. Here are some examples:

PRO's

- I'll look forward to getting up in the morning and feel energized
- I can see a career pathway and journey for my future
- I won't have to work with this team/manager
- I'll be excited and challenged
- More money*

CON's

- I'll have to go through the process of applying and interviewing
- It's scary to think of a new job in a new team/company
- I might not get the job
- I've been here for years and will lose the benefits

It's also beneficial to list the Pro's and Con's of your current role to assist you in this decision making of 'should I look for another job or stay where I am?'.

Now, lists are great if you do something with them. You've listed the reasons why you're looking for a new job, the pro's and con's of a new job, and your current job, and if you feel you're still wanting to secure that new role, you need to now list/think of the positive aspects to the Con's you've listed and begin to 'get in the right mindset' of positive excitement of getting a new job and all the Pro's you'll get to enjoy.

*I would recommend almost ignoring the money aspect until the very last point you think of. More money is not a good reason to secure a new job on its own, trust me. I've seen it many many times over the years "I'm going to take this job over here as it pays more money" a month goes by and I receive a call "Is that other job still available? The culture/job isn't what I expected". This is because when money is the main driver or it's extremely attractive, people forget to consider whether it's the right role, company, team and manager/s for them and just think of the $'s.

MINDSET

Think about the process of getting a new job, and ultimately starting a new job in a new company/team.

Are you prepared to put the time and effort into 'putting your best foot forward'? or are you just going to click apply and cross your fingers? If it's the latter, put the book down and spend time with yourself thinking about the above again and if you're really dedicated to getting a new job.

I know it's 'easier said than done' but YOU CAN DO IT! You are the best you there is.

You need to believe in yourself and have confidence that you do your job well and deserve better, the best!
  If this isn't the case (doing your job well), then as mentioned above, spend time with yourself 'evaluating' your performance and what you can and should be doing to be the best at your job/version of yourself.

3

TRADITIONAL RECRUITMENT / APPLICATION PROCESS

The traditional/usual recruitment process might look something like this:

- Company advertises position
- Apply and upload your CV/Cover Letter
- Never hear from them again

OR

- Company advertises position
- Apply and upload your CV/Cover Letter
- Get shortlisted
- Screening call or Email to say you've been selected
- Interview

Sometimes there is no way to avoid the traditional recruitment process... however, I do truly believe that you can influence it. Firstly, by focusing and spending time crafting a CV and Cover Letter - the Cover Letter is up to you or the information you can find out about the organization and if they like/prefer it or not, Secondly, making connections* (via LinkedIn or personal networks) that may be able to swing the needle a little more so in your favor, and lastly to nail the interview of course.

*To give context, imagine you're a hiring manager and you receive a large amount of applications/CV's either directly or via your TA/Recruitment/HR team/s, you have to spend time reading/viewing these and making a decision who you should interview, but wait a minute, they recognize the name as you sent a personalized, well written LinkedIn connection request/message or someone has given them/you a highly regarded recommendation, automatically your name stands out and makes them focus slightly more on your CV/Cover letter/application. There it is, the 1% we're looking for!

4

YOUR CV

T his is one of the main, and dare I say only, places in the world where you should be promoting yourself and how good you are. There are many ways to format a CV and if you speak with recruitment and career advice professionals, you'll most probably get a different opinion from each, but also with hiring managers and Talent Acquisition teams too. So, you have to make your own decision based on information you gather, and run with it.

Here's a few key things that I would highly recommend having in it though:

- **Personal details**, such as Name, Mobile, Town/City/Suburb (not full address), email address

- **Summary** - 1 paragraph summarizing who you are, what you stand for and a few key aspects to your career. For example; I am an adaptable, challenge focused person who always strives to be the best version of myself, through constant professional and personal development. I have been a recruitment specialist for 15+ years within one of the world's largest (Global Fortune 500) HR & Recruitment Services providers, and recruited in many different industries, including; Education, HR, Banking & Finance and Technology

- **Technical Skills and/or Education** – Degrees and recognized industry certifications (especially if they are relevant to the job/company you're applying to)
- If you have a number of years experience across a number of companies, it's worth putting a **career snapshot** in eg. A table of Company, Job Title, Dates you worked there

- **Career history** – This should give a quick 1 line overview of what company you worked for so that the reader knows what the company does, it's not good to assume everyone knows every company and what they do. Below this there should be a short section of bullet points (approx 5x) of your role content and below this I'd recommend an Achievements section to showcase how well you did your role against your peers for example; In 2019 I was part of a small team of 3 people that designed, created, implemented and deployed the national on-boarding program, which 150+ people each year go through

- As you'll see in the example below, it's sometimes beneficial to **break up your experience** within a position into smaller sections, but I recommend this if it has varied responsibilities, such as; leading a team, bids & tenders, account management/business development, different programs or projects etc

- **Additional professional and personal development** courses and/or certificates you've obtained. Similar to previously, I would recommend that they are somewhat current and relevant. There's no point in putting that you completed your level 5 Sea Turtle swim school certificate, unless your job would entail having this of course

- **References** - I believe that this is a given to most positions and there's no longer a reason to list people or even that they are 'Available upon request'. I've seen that some people list their referees personal details here, but what I imagine has and could happen is that your CV is put on someone's desk and/or could land in the wrong hands, and you've just given out other people's mobile/email details ready for potential spamming name

Email:

Phone:

Mobile:

IT Management | IT Strategy | ERP | Stakeholder Management | Transformation

Proven National IT & Business Systems Manager with over 15 years experience in IT Applications, infrastructure Management. Responsible for multi-site management across all aspects of hardware, software and peripherals. Recognised strategic leader with demonstrated capabilities in project management (Prince2 & PMBOK), vendor engagement, contract negotiation and policy development driving innovative solutions to meet dynamic business conditions. Recognised industry specialist responsible for implementing key methodologies for business improvement,

KEY SKILLS SUMMARY

- Business Transformation
- Strategic Planning and management
- Project leadership | Project Management
- Infrastructure design | Planning
- Risk management | Mitigation planning
- Disaster recovery strategies
- Policy development
- Team mentoring | Leadership
- Supplier negotiation
- SDLC
- Vendor/Contract management

- IT Operations Management
- Change Management
- Budget management
- Quality control
- Process improvement
- Key stakeholder management
- ERP – Oracle, Dynamics AX, SAP B1
- Business Analysis
- CRM; SAP, Peoplesoft, Salesforce
- IT Governance | ITIL
- Cloud Technologies; AWS, AZURE

TECHNICAL SKILLS SUMMARY

Applications	Advanced Access, Project, Word, Excel, PowerPoint, Visio, SharePoint
Databases	MS-SQL, Ingress II, Progress, Oracle,
ERP	Oracle eBusiness, MS Dynamics AX 2009, SAP B1, MAPICS, BPCS, MK, BAAN, MFGPro, Design of Bespoke Systems to meet specific business Needs, including Manufacturing Shop Floor, quality control, Poka Yoke & PLC integration
Operating Systems	Microsoft NT, 2K, XP, 2007, Vista, Windows 8
Server Environments	Windows 2k, 2003, 2008, Virtualisation, Deployment of hosted environments, VMware, Citrix
Workflow / Shop floor / Point Of Sale	Lotus Notes Development / Administration, SharePoint, PLC integration, Barcode Applications, RF Smart, Microsoft AX Retail POS, ProMapp
Industries	Manufacturing, Automotive, Printing, Government, Retail, Apparel, Distribution, Logistics.

EMPLOYMENT SUMMARY

XXXXXXX	XXXXX	July 2016 - Current
XXXXXXX	XXXXXXXXXXX	Mar 2005 – Mar 2016
XXXXXXX	XXXXXXXXXXXX	Jan 2004 – Mar 2005
XXXXXXX	XXXXXXX	Nov 1999 – Dec 2003
XXXXXXX	XXXXXXXXXXX	Dec 1996 – Oct 1999
XXXXXXX	XXXXXXX	Nov 1995 – March 1996
XXXXXXXX	XXXXXX	Jul 1994 – Feb 1995
XXXXXXX	XXXXX	Jul 1992 – Jul 1994

EMPLOYMENT HISTORY

XXCOMPANY NAME XXX   JULY 2016 – CURRENT

XXXXX was established in XXX, and is Australia's leading XXXXXXX.

HEAD OF IT   JULY 2016 – CURRENT

Leadership: Full responsibility for the mentoring, recruitment, performance management, and salary review of 10+ full time personnel; Including Business Analysts, Infrastructure Engineers, Process Improvement Engineers
Annual Budget Accountability: AU$4.5 Million
Reporting Line: Senior Manager Level reporting to the CEO/Founder/Owner of XXX
Projects: Responsible for restoring reliability, and transforming a poor ERP implementation into a business enabler. Development of the roadmap including the successful completion of multiple strategic initiatives.

Contributions and Achievements

- Responsible for managing the XXX thematic goal of "Restoring Reliability".

  o Designed and Implemented the Sales and Operation planning (S&OP) Process, which included the selection and implementation of a software solution for Forecasting and Demand Planning.
  o Correction of Data Integrity issues and implementation of validation throughout all systems including Point of Sale and Internet platform.
  o Redefinition and streamlining of business workflows
  o Resolution of business critical bugs relating to Microsoft Dynamics AX ERP and POS.

- Implementation of Demand Solutions – Forecasting, Demand Management and National Replenishment.

  o Investigated and recommended solution, including preparation of proposal, and project management and full implementation from end to end.
  o Realized the key benefit of providing XXX with the visibility to plan stock based on an intelligent forecast, incorporating adjusted history, market intelligence, and supersession information
  o Full integration with Microsoft AX (Company wide ERP) and BI Reporting
  o Provided company with detailed analysis of SLOB (Slow moving and obsolete)
  o Delivered ability to produce upstream 12 month schedules to local and overseas suppliers.
  o Reduction in backorder position, and air freight costs resulting from improved purchasing process and incorporation of minimum order quantities and correct lead times.

- Implementation of ProMapp – Business Process Mapping software

  o Identification and documentation of all company wide business processes
  o Establishment of a governance framework to manage changes and improvements

- Managed strategic decision to Migrate AX Support to alternative supplier

  o Successful Risk mitigation relating to the decommissioning of existing support provider
  o Managed due-diligence, selection process, and seamless transition of incoming partner

- Managed and lead other transformational activities including:

  o Transition of Microsoft AX ERP Infrastructure to Cloud Services (Telstra)
  o Implementation of RF Smart Warehouse intelligence to provide real time performance reports
  o Implementation of EDI processing of internet orders eliminating manual process and elimination of returns due to keying errors
  o Implementation of Smart email functionality providing internal and external alerts and informative emails notifying customers of order status.
  o Redeployment, Data Cleansing and restructuring BI Data Warehouse Cubes used for efficiently feeding SSRS Reporting and Targit BI Reporting
  o Implemented IP Telephony Solution including Service Desk and Contact Centre

- Improved the reputation and culture of the systems department

  o Creating ownership and an outcome focused team with measurable key performance indicators.
  o Implementation of ITIL and an IT Governance framework to manage change control, helpdesk, asset management and system access.

QUALIFICATIONS

- XXXXX
- XXXXXX

PROFESSIONAL DEVELOPMENT & CERTIFICATES

SAP B1 Administration / Implementation
Oracle eBusiness Admin
Oracle eBusiness Financials
Oracle Discovery Reports
Microsoft AX 2009 – Production
Project management (PMBOK)
Leadership and Management
Time Management
Handling Uncertainty, Stress & Anxiety
Working together as a team
Communication and Negotiation Skills
Performance Management
Leverage Business Strategy with IT
Just in Time Workshop (APICS)
Lotus Notes Admin and Development
MK Ingress DBA 1 & 2
SQL 2000/2003/2008 Development
VB.Net Development

* I will highlight that as you see, this is an example CV for an IT Manager, and it may not be specifically suited to your industry, so think about the key things that any manager/employer will want to see. Not that you won 2nd place in your primary school cross country race (I have actually seen this exact example from a person who has lots of experience and was at school 25+ years ago).

Don't be afraid of asking advice from someone who works at the company or in the industry you're applying to, they may have some tips that can assist further in 'putting your best foot forward.

5

COVER LETTER

Cover letters sometimes have a love/hate relationship with the reader. They read it and love/hate it, or don't read it at all. I think it's an opportunity, outside of the CV of course, to speak directly to the reader, whether they actually read it or not of course, so why not take the opportunity to do so in case they do read it?

Granted, some organizations/people would like this to be a professional addressing of the key selection criteria, which is something through networking and calling to ask that you may be able to find out, from an organization perspective at least, however, most people who read the cover letters are just like you and I, they are looking to connect with the person behind the CV/cover letter. I believe, and through my 15+ years of experience internationally, that interviews and job opportunities are 10% CV/Cover letter and 90% the person, so why not give yourself an additional 1% ahead of the pack if they do read the cover letter.

Here's an example which I wrote as if I were applying for an IT Manager position:

James Sycamore
Melbourne, Australia
T: +61 123456789
E: youremailaddress@gmail.com

Dear Penny and the team at XYZ Ltd.

Thank you for taking the time to read my cover letter, CV and application.
It's with great pleasure and excitement that I write to you in regards to the position of IT Manager at XYZ Ltd.
Having worked as an IT Manager at XXXCompany NameXXX for almost 7 years and utilizing similar technology, to build and lead a team whereby a culture of collaboration, partnership and respect is now the norm, and the team have become very efficient, self-sufficient and high performing, I believe it's time for me to take on a new challenge.

From what I understand of XYZ Ltd and the insights I've gained from the industry, I believe that the business and people there match my values of the above, mixed with the motivation to provide excellent service to both internal and external stakeholders and customers, which truly excites me.

As you'll read from my CV, accolades and achievements, it's my view that there aren't many people in Melbourne who would be better suited to leading the team to further success there. Granted, I may still have a bit to learn, but I can guarantee that you won't find anyone who is more passionate, dedicated and driven to do this to the highest of standards than me.

I hope that we have the opportunity to meet and get to know one another, and I highly appreciate the chance to be considered for this outstanding position.

I look forward to any questions and shaking your hand in the near future.

Thanks and warm regards,
James

6

LINKEDIN

WHAT IS LINKEDIN?

LinkedIn is a professional social media platform that has over 1 billion members in over 200 countries, which is owned by Microsoft.

So if you're not on it, then it's definitely worth looking into. Granted, there are some industries, jobs and people that don't use it, but I (almost) guarantee that it can potentially improve an aspect of the application process to help get your dream job. It is also widely used as a tool to 'check out' or research an applicant and see how they present themselves, prior to even considering if they are right for the job and worth interviewing.

There are other social media platforms that your industry might use that can help you secure your dream job, but I'm sorry to say, I'm not your expert on these. LinkedIn is our daily 'go to' within the recruitment industry.

HOW TO USE IT

Imagine Facebook, Instagram, Twitter all rolled into one. You can scroll the feed for interesting posts and articles, create your own content - write an article, post your thoughts, share links and web pages, post/like photos and videos (and create them / live videos), follow and connect with people - with a messenger function, follow companies, join groups and more.

My top tips:

- If you're using it, use it - what I mean by this is have a picture, background cover photo, career dates, summary and complete all aspects of your profile AT LEAST
- Connect with people you know or have worked with
- Follow companies you like or would like to work for, and even competition companies so it can give you insights into what the company you're going for might be looking to or needing to do to stay competitive and at the forefront of the industry
- Follow and connect with people in your industry or within jobs similar to yours
- Engage with the content you see. Like, comment, repost and create

*I may have to write another book specifically on this topic, so I would love to hear your feedback and thoughts if this would be useful?

7

RECRUITMENT AGENCY / RECRUITER RELATIONSHIPS

Recruiters, love us or hate us, we can bring lots of value to your application process, and we're happy to, well most of us, the good ones at least. There are hundreds, if not, thousands out there, and you may align with some, but not all, because they may not work in your industry, and even you may not 'like' the look and feel of the company/people there, and this isn't a bad thing. You want to, and need to, feel fully comfortable and confident that they are the 'right partners' for you.

What I mean by this is that naturally, like in everyday life, you will get along with some people and won't with others. You'll like the look of companies and not others too. Like grabbing a coffee, if the shop looks appealing, it's busy/has a good reputation, and the people are nice and welcoming, you'll be more likely to go in and get a coffee, and go back again. The same is for recruitment agencies, so ask around and start introducing yourself to them.

Trust me though, you'll soon find out who the good ones are by as little as whether you can find their details easily, call and get in touch, with a reply within 24-48 hours. Sadly, a large number will either not be easy to connect/speak with and won't respond to your call. The reason I say call is so that you can actually speak with the person/people at the other end and start building a true partnership/relationship. This is key to being able to find your dream position, if you're going via a recruiter of course. It's not essential, but they can help in a BIG way.

If you don't believe me, call a recruiter to connect (hopefully they'll pick up, but it may take trying a few different companies though, sorry!) and understand who they are, which industries they recruit in, and how they may be able to assist you...then, whilst you're talking with them, ask 'have you heard of XYZ Ltd? What are your thoughts on them? How are people who work there perceived in the market?'

You'll soon understand the ins and outs of the company you may be interested in applying to, but also, if you build relationships with a handful of recruiters that you connect with on a personal level, at some point they will potentially call you with your dream job or have it available then and there.

As recruiters you must understand that we may not have 'the ideal/your dream job' for you when you're thinking of moving, the key is to build the relationships prior to wanting to leave so when your dream job comes across their desk, they call you! To make the most out of your relationships with recruiter, and assist them in helping YOU, make sure to:

- Be transparent about you, your career and CV, reasons for looking, leaving previous jobs, shoe size etc. (Kidding about the last one, but you get the picture)

- Work with them to uncover your 'ideal, 'must haves', 'like to have' and minimum expectations
- Communication, communication, communication, without this the relationship will fall down. Have other interviews, let them know, in fact, ask their advice. As I said before, the good ones will help you. Not sure about something, nervous for the interview, whatever it is, and again, the good ones will help you.

8

PRIOR TO A PRE-SCREENING CALL

It's not often, but you may get a call to discuss your application prior to being selected for an interview, and this is your chance to 'showcase' your personality and experience, but be careful to not go too in-depth as it may scare people off. The key is to have done your homework, know why you're interested in this position, the company, and a little about what you know - this doesn't have to take hours, just checking their website, values, mission statement and really thinking about why you want to work for them, before applying.

Also, I know it may sound silly, but imagine them calling you. Walk through the conversation in your head and even out loud and imagine the conversation flow/how you'll answer their questions - 'what made you apply to this position? Why now? Why us/this company/this role? Why should we consider you?' I'm not saying to spend hours in front of the mirror, but I do know that 'people will rarely remember what you say, they will mainly remember how you make them feel' so practice it, think of the words you use, are they positive? Ensure that your tone and pitch are energetic, head held high vs looking down, all the key 'sales tactics'.

If you're not aware of 'sales tactics', it helps massively by smiling and being positive/happy when on the phone, and ultimately it's about promoting value and benefits in a positive and exciting way, not manipulation like most people think it is.

Another checklist for you:

- Do you know about the company you're applying to, their history, values, mission statement, countries they operate in, size, products/services, # of employees locally/nationally/globally
- Why do you want this job, with this company? How will you articulate this?
- Ideally where possible, coordinate the time so you can be comfortable, relaxed and ready for their call
- Think of further questions they may ask; What skills and expertise will you bring to this role and company? 'tell me about yourself...'**,
- Prepare some questions! What's the manager/team like? How long have you been there and why do you like working there? How do you think my skills, experience and personality stack up against other applicants? Do you think there's anything I'm missing or will need to develop on?

**I could write another book on this topic, but in short, be yourself, genuine and authentic, but make sure to 'SELL YOURSELF' and be confident/energetic. Practice your 30-60 second elevator pitch (If you've not heard of this term, imagine being in an elevator and meeting someone and they ask this question, you have only a few floors to get your point across in a positive and way that they'll remember) eg. I'm a recruitment specialist and have been for over 15 years now, and I love getting to connect great people with just as great companies in the Technology industry everyday, what do you do?

9

PRE-INTERVIEW PREPARATION

Make sure you **know the details,** I'm going to do it...put in another list for you:

- What date/day/time is the interview?
- Is it on-site/face-to-face or online?
- Do you have the address/have you tested the link and downloaded any upgrades to the application?
- Will it be 1on1 or a panel interview?
- Are there 1 or more stages?
- What should you wear?
- Do you need to bring or present anything?
- What will the structure of the interview be? How long is the interview planned for?

Homework, there's not a huge amount of people that like doing homework whilst at school, but it is essential prior to any interview. Further to the above points, doing your research into the company, and the

25

role again - checking the key aspects that stand out of a Position Description/Advertisement and thinking of succinct (1-2 paragraphs/30-60 seconds) examples where you've done or are doing what they're needing/looking for - answer these using the STAR* method, the person you are meeting - now that you have a LinkedIn account you can search the person and where they work and pick out a couple of things to ask/show that you've done your research, such as; they've been at the company 10 years - you should ask 'what do they like/love about working there? What did they find the biggest hurdles they faced throughout their career there?' 'If you were to be successful, is there any advice they would give you?' - I really like these types of questions at interviews, especially if you're building good rapport with the person as you're talking as if you could, or are going to be working there.

Practice the way you will answer the BBI (Behavioral Based Interview) questions, out loud. I cannot stress how good it is to practice this out loud, and yes, it might feel silly but it's a key aspect to the interview. How confident you are and sharing specific examples that align to what they are looking for/needing in this role, and key it showcases your communication skills, that let's be honest, is essential to a large portion of positions that exist.

On this note, **write everything down**, but DO NOT read it whilst in the interview, it just helps the brain cement the information when you write things down, and you need to also write down a number of questions that you want to ask the interviewer/s too.

DO NOT FORGET, **you are also interviewing them**. Are they someone you want to work with/for, is it the type of role/company you want to work in etc.

Questions - It can be detrimental when they ask "do you have any questions?" and you say no. A better answer to this is always, "well I had written down a number of questions here on my pad (and potentially show them briefly too), but we've actually covered them off during our conversation, thank you.", and if you haven't this is your chance to ask, but not having any in the first place shows them that you either do not prepare or maybe even really care about the interview/getting the job.

Goals/Future aspirations - What are your short term and long term career goals? What do you hope to achieve in this position/company and into the future?

How will you finish the interview and what are the next steps?

This is something that most people tend to forget, especially in the heat of the moment. Plan how you're going to thank the interview panel for their time and the opportunity to meet them/be considered for the position.

Ask if they have any further questions or would like to go over anything again/in more depth?

Is there any specific feedback they could give to you on your interview? - This shows a potential employer that you are proactive in asking for feedback and looking for areas to improve.

If you were to be successful, what and when are the next stages?

What are your strengths and development areas?

Know them both and plan how you're going to provide examples or explain them in the interview. If you're not sure, ask your manager/colleagues, partner, friends and/or family.

DO NOT shy away from knowing your areas for development and discussing them, but you do need to put them in a somewhat positive light of course eg. 'I have a tendency to greatly care about the standards of my work, so occasionally I go into more depth than I need to, however, I openly discuss this with my manager/s and team to ensure I know what depth I need to go into and time frames/deadlines required, which I ensure I meet and exceed.'

You know I love a list by now:

- Interview details
- Homework/research
- Imagine the questions or flow of the interview
- Practice your answers
- Write everything down but do not rehearse the exact words you will use
- What questions you're going to ask and how
- Finishing the interview
- Strengths and development areas

***STAR**

SITUATION - Set the scene for the interviewer as to the situation/event/challenge you faced

TASK - What the task was that you and/or the team had to work through

ACTION - What steps did YOU take to get the desired outcome/result

RESULT - What did you achieve by the actions you took?

You should use this as a good way to structure your answers to their potential questions, and remember you can't be completely ready for every question they might ask, but doing preparation for a few of them helps for you to build confidence that you're ready for any question they throw at you.

10

THE INTERVIEW

So you've written a great CV/Cover Letter, had a pre-screening call, prepared for the interview and are now at the big day.

Relax, it's just 2 or more humans meeting to see if they like each other, if they can use your experience at the company they work for, but also that you like them/the role/company.

PLEASE DO NOT FORGET... You are in the driving seat of your career and have the power to do well, say yes or no to this position, but without all the previous aspects clicking into place prior you wouldn't be in this situation, so be proud of getting to this stage, whatever the outcome, and also remember that you only have 1 chance to make a first impression, so make it count.

- You're either early or you're late. **Be early, don't be late.** Make sure you plan and map out your journey, then leave 30-60 minutes early to ensure if there's anything that goes wrong on your journey, you have time. This also counts for online interviews, but you may not need as much time of course. Test the link/your camera/mic, check your background is tidy/presentable, make sure you're fed and watered beforehand, you have your notes/questions, you're smartly dressed and look presentable, have a glass of water to hand (we'll come to this shortly) and breathe. Take 5 large breaths in, hold it, and out again. If all goes to plan you could be in your new job after this, be excited about that rather than worrying about the process to get there. As I mentioned before, we're all human, so don't put extra pressure on yourself to be perfect, no-one is perfect and ever will be

- **Smile and give a firm, but not hard, handshake**. There's no better (or worse) start to an interview than a confident, positive welcome and handshake. Skin on skin is still a very valuable greeting to an interview, and if you're online, there's no harm in a wave to go with your smile too

- Be **confident** in yourself and your experience/skills, and remember there's no other person exactly like you!

- If you're **nervous**, be open about it. Again, you are human. You can put a positive spin on it though 'Apologies if I seem a bit nervous, I am, but also very excited to be considered for this position'

- **Listen carefully** to the interview panel's questions and make sure you answer their actual question, and if you're not quite sure, ask

- **Body language**, we have to talk about this as we all know that actions/expressions sometimes speak louder than words. Be very conscious of your mannerisms, expressions and reactions to questions or how you answer them too, tone and energy. Speak with enthusiasm and do not shy away from using gestures and your hands when you speak, especially in online interviews. I cannot count the number of times I have come away from an interview feeling like the person didn't care just because of the lack of enthusiasm and passion they show through the screen, but also the other way around. If someone is genuine and excited/engaging, I have walked away thinking 'wow, I really liked their energy'.

Here's a few tips to remember:

- Sit up straight, don't slouch or become too relaxed/lean back
- Maintain eye contact
- Don't fidget or move too much
- Keep smiling, not awkwardly of course, try to be as natural as possible
- Be aware of your expressions and passion/excitement
- Talk to, and maintain eye contact with everyone, don't stare

- **Take your time** to formulate an answer, there's no harm in some silence or as mentioned before, to buy yourself a bit of thinking time, take a sip of water. The panel isn't expecting you to answer straight away, with the perfect answer, they are just looking to see how you react to the question and approach the answer. Most people will not remember the exact words you say, but how you make them feel, so as highlighted before, be confident, engaging and succinct, you can always ask them again, 'is that what you were looking for?/did I give a good example for your question?'

· **Speak positively**. Aim to never speak negatively about a situation, experience or person, even if it was a terrible one, you can always keep it positive, for example; 'It wasn't the most enjoyable experience, however, I learned so much about..."

· **Talk to everyone there**, maintaining eye contact with the person who asked the question, but also making sure that you also engage/switch your eyes to others in the room. There's nothing worse than only focusing on the person asking the question/s. You will naturally look at/answer them, however, don't forget to include the other person/people in the room. If you don't, they will come away saying 'They didn't acknowledge me in the interview' and this will be very tough to counteract once the interview is over

· Throughout the interview, be conscious of **how much depth** you're going into. I am quite aware that sometimes I will become passionate about a topic and ramble on, so I always look to bring myself back to the original question and simply answer it, if this has occurred. If you aren't sure if you're someone who goes into too much depth, ask the people closest to you - colleagues, manager/s, friends, family etc

- You want to make sure that you're not **losing their attention**, so referring to the panel by their names will help to continue to engage everyone there, and keep the conversation both ways by asking 'off the cuff' questions as you move along the conversation eg. 'Whilst working at ABC Co I did XZY (insert STAR structure to their question) and I see that you, Penny, also worked within the JKL industry, how did you find it?'

- Don't be afraid of highlighting your **strengths and development areas** as you go along the interview, and if you haven't done something before or know the answer, as we discussed before, there's no harm in showing you're human, no one is perfect - "I'm not sure about that/I've never done/experienced that before, but in that situation I would ask you/the team, do some research and find out more about it so I could approach it with more knowledge and potentially do XYZ." This is another situation where "I don't know or haven't done it" will be detrimental to your success in the interview. It's always better to offer a solution to a problem, even if it's 'I'll do my research/ask'

· As the interview wraps up, **thank the panel** for the opportunity to meet again and for being considered for the position

· As mentioned above, it's good to **'pulse check'** with the panel to make sure that they have everything they need – "Is there anything you wanted me to go into further depth on?"

· If you have genuinely enjoyed meeting them and the interview/hearing about the role and company, **tell them how you feel**! I always use this analogy – if you were at a BBQ and 2 people you'd just met said "It was nice to chat, see you next time" & "It was great chatting and I really enjoyed meeting you, thanks for the chat." Who are you more likely to want to meet again just from this comment? There's only benefit to saying "Thanks very much for the opportunity to meet you all and be considered for the position, I'm really excited at the prospect of working with you, Penny, and the team, it sounds like you have a great culture, good values that align very well with mine and I can see that if I were to join you, I'd enjoy it and be able to become an integral part of the team and develop a successful, long lasting career here." – I will add to this that it does of course depend on the position you are going for, if it's a temporary contract it may slightly differ what you say here as you won't of course develop a long lasting career there, but you get the gist

· Even if you haven't enjoyed the interview it's always best to thank them for their time of course

- Keep an **eye on the time**, if you're getting close to the end of the allotted time, say "I know we're getting close to the end of the interview, am I OK to ask…" depending on the situation and time of course. There's also no harm in saying "I do have a few additional questions or would like to understand a little more about ABC, but I know we're short on time, would you mind or potentially have time for a quick chat again after this?" It will show the panel that you can be good at time keeping and self aware as to both yours, and other people's time

- **Ask what and when** you'll hear about the next steps and if it's OK to keep in touch. Naturally people are busy, and some organizations have strict processes around interviews and next steps/communication

- Some are good and sadly, a large amount are not when it comes to feedback, especially when you aren't successful. It's good to ask this question as they will (most of the time) be happy for you to keep in touch so after the 'you'll hear back next week' time frame has passed, they have given you permission to reach out/stay in touch

11

POST INTERVIEW

T hank them again. Whoever arranged the interview, and also the interviewing panel. Send an email to say thanks for the opportunity to meet/interview and that you're excited by the opportunity and why. An example could be as simple as:

'Hi Penny & John, thank you both very much for the opportunity to meet you and for the chance to join your team/s at ABC Ltd. I'm excited at the prospect of this position and working with you all at ABC Ltd, I can see it giving me the opportunity to further develop my skills and knowledge in XYZ whilst working within a team that seems to be very collaborative, supportive and fun too, additionally, from what you've told me about the culture there, I feel I could become a high performing team member in the position within a short amount of time.

I look forward to hearing the outcome/next steps next week (or whenever they said they would), and would greatly appreciate any and all feedback, whether positive or otherwise.

Hope to speak soon, and if there's anything further you require or would like to ask, please call me on 0123456789 or email js@made-upemail.com.au.'

1. THINGS TO REMEMBER AND MISTAKES TO AVOID...

- Be yourself, a genuine, authentic, honest YOU!
- Plan for the interview, but prepare to be thrown off course and how you'll deal with it
- Don't be a robot with your answers or read word-for-word from your notes
- Open up the cupboard to your strengths and development areas
- To reiterate, people will rarely remember what you said, but how you make them feel - enjoy yourself, truly get to know the person/people you're meeting.

Send LinkedIn connection requests to everyone you met and spoke with throughout the process and again, thank them for the opportunity to meet.

That's it. Pat yourself on the back and look forward to the good news, or at least some feedback on areas where you can improve. I say at least, however, sadly you may not receive any feedback, just a yes or no answer, and you shouldn't take this personally.

Most organizations have HR or Talent Acquisition teams that manage the process and next steps, and they may not know to ask for feedback or get it from the interview panel. I'm not making excuses for people, because it should be a minimum standard for everyone during an interview process to receive feedback so they can improve, but I know from many years of experience that this may not always happen.

Either way, you should be proud of following all these steps and doing your best throughout the process and interview. It's tough and will not often be a 'walk in the park' when it comes to interviews, so well done!

12

CONCLUSION

Try your best to enjoy the process. Make sure to remind yourself that as much as it may be your dream job, there's plenty of other opportunities and companies out there, this isn't your one and only chance there ever will be. Unless you join and stay for your entire career, which isn't necessarily a good or a bad thing, then you will most probably have other jobs that come up over the years, so make sure you ENJOY IT!

Enjoy meeting new people, enjoy nailing a certain question or more, enjoy learning from one that you didn't, enjoy building your LinkedIn network should it not work out. As long as you are pleasant, respectful and present yourself in the best way you can, there's nothing more anyone or you can ask of yourself.

Congratulations on getting this far. You should feel proud of yourself!

I look forward to hearing all about the amazing, and not so amazing interviews you all have. Which tips helped you the most and even where I can improve or add to this book to make it even better too. I love feedback, positive or otherwise.

If you've found this book helpful and learned a thing or 2, I'd really appreciate a favorable review on Amazon, and a HUGE THANKS again for purchasing and reading my book. Keep an eye out for others coming in the near future!

13

RESOURCES

About LinkedIn. (n.d.). About LinkedIn. https://about.linkedin.com/#:~:text=About%20LinkedIn&text=1%20billion%20members%20join%20more,member%20of%20the%20global%20workforce.&text=The%20mission%20of%20LinkedIn%20is,them%20more%20productive%20and%20successful.

Preparing for a job interview - tips | Reed.co.uk. (n.d.). reed.co.uk. https://www.reed.co.uk/career-advice/interview-techniques/preparing-for-a-job-interview/

SEEK Limited. (2022, February 4). Interview preparation checklist. SEEK. https://www.seek.com.au/career-advice/article/how-to-prepare-for-your-interview-the-ultimate-guide

Australia, R. (n.d.). interview tips. https://www.randstad.com.au/job-seekers/job-seeker-toolkit/interview-tips/